I See You

A Guide to Finding Your Inner Strength,
Confidence, and Voice After Trauma and Abuse

Jennifer J. Boutwell

BALBOA.PRESS
A DIVISION OF HAY HOUSE

Balboa Press books may be ordered through booksellers or by contacting:

Balboa Press
A Division of Hay House
1663 Liberty Drive
Bloomington, IN 47403
www.balboapress.com
844-682-1282

Print information available on the last page.

ISBN: 979-8-7652-5822-4 (sc)
ISBN: 979-8-7652-5821-7 (hc)
ISBN: 979-8-7652-5820-0 (e)

Library of Congress Control Number: 2024925720

Balboa Press rev. date: 12/10/2024

Contents

Introduction ix

Chapter 1 Taking Back My Life 1
Chapter 2 Embracing the Waves of Grief:
          A Journey of Healing, Synchronicity, and
          Self-Discovery 7
Chapter 3 Look Within to Your Purpose 13
Chapter 4 Finding My Confidence 21
Chapter 5 Unconditional Love Starts with Loving
          Yourself 29
Chapter 6 Letting Go of Limiting Beliefs and
          Affirming the Life of Your Dreams 53
Chapter 7 The Power of Forgiveness 65
Chapter 8 The Power of Your Inner Circle:
          Building a Team for Personal and
          Professional Growth 75
Chapter 9 My Future Self 83

Special Thanks 89
Bibliography 91

To my baby sister, Gabrielle "Gabby" Boutwell (June 18, 1998 – April 29, 2022). At 4 foot 11, you were proof that big things come in small packages. A spitfire with a heart of gold, a force to be reckoned with, you lived fiercely and fearlessly. As a paramedic, you dedicated your life to saving others, and even in your passing, your generosity continued as you gave the gift of life through organ donation. You were small but mighty, a force of nature who left an unforgettable legacy of strength, and love. Gabby, you are forever in my heart, and this book is a tribute to your incredible spirit and the light you brought to the world. I have no doubt that you are a sword toting angel stirring up some ruckus in heaven.

Introduction

When the idea of writing a book first took hold of my heart, I was flooded with questions. Despite the uncertainty, I knew I had to do it. I didn't even know where to begin, so I dove into researching everything about writing and publishing. That journey led me to a Hay House event called "I Can Do It" in Tampa, Florida. It was there, sitting in a room full of like-minded souls, that I first heard Gabrielle Bernstein speak. I left her session with a deep conviction: not only was I meant to write this book, but I also needed to take her writing class.

Years of journaling had already set the foundation, though I hadn't realized it at the time. Gabrielle spoke about the power of life experiences, and the importance of listening to your intuition and recognizing those messages as whispers from Spirit. A year later, I found myself at another Hay House conference, listening to Gabrielle again. This time, her words about forgiveness and the understanding that not everyone will grow with us resonated deeply. Accepting this truth became part of my journey.

The purpose of this book is to empower others who have found themselves in situations like mine. I want to reach those who have felt unworthy, undeserving, or even unlovable.

My wish is that each reader will discover self-acceptance, strength, value, confidence, and, most importantly, a deep love from within. I want you to see your greatness, to love yourself for who you are. We all deserve an extraordinary human experience filled with unconditional love. My hope is that this book will serve as a guide to help you break free from narcissistic, abusive relationships and heal the wounds and trauma that life can bring.

Abuse comes in many forms. When I started researching abuse, I was shocked at the variety: physical, sexual, mental, elderly, bullying, religious, child, verbal—the list goes on. I've personally experienced several of these, sometimes without even realizing it at the time. Abuse doesn't always come from a romantic partner or a parent; it can come from society, religions, or even friends.

In my journey, I've faced abuse from different sources, and I will share these experiences in this book. One relationship in particular was the most damaging, because it involved verbal and mental abuse. It was a narcissistic relationship where everyone was put down and made to feel insignificant. Through the techniques, behaviors, and therapies I'll share with you, I've been able to reclaim myself and heal.

I've learned that narcissistic relationships often stem from the beliefs we were taught or conditioned to hold about ourselves. When you remove these false beliefs and start seeing yourself as the beautiful soul you truly are, you can begin to love yourself. You can heal your inner child, find your inner strength, and become your higher self. You are an amazing human with something incredibly special to contribute to the universe. All you must do is stop believing the conditioned lies about yourself. You are an amazing soul. You are love. You deserve all the love there is. Here's to finding your true inner voice, strength, and confidence to love yourself.

At the age of forty-nine, as my third marriage was coming to an end, I found myself sitting on a beach in the rain, mourning a relationship that had left me broken and filled with self-doubt. For eight long years, my children and I had walked on eggshells. I felt like I couldn't even fold a towel correctly.

On the outside, people saw a happy couple—two ambitious individuals working toward their goals. But behind closed doors, our relationship was humiliating and painful. I am an intelligent, successful woman. I own and lead a thriving salon company. I've organized and volunteered for numerous nonprofit events and fundraisers. I have the privilege of leading a team of consultants across four states and working as a coach with more than twenty-five accounts. And yet, here I was, facing another divorce, trying to figure out where I lost myself.

When did I lose control of my life? When did I lose my confidence? My voice? How was I silenced? How did I end up in this situation? How did I allow this to happen to my two boys? And to me? I had stayed for far too long. Why?

My ego and pride played a part—I didn't want to go through another divorce. I didn't want my kids to go through another divorce. I worried about what people would say. Why did I care what they said? I knew that leaving would make life hell, worse than what I was already living through. I knew he would try to take everything I had worked for. There would be smear campaigns, lies, and manipulation. How could I escape with the least number of casualties?

In August, my youngest son and I evacuated for a hurricane. For three weeks, we were away from home, and life was easy—peaceful even. When we returned, my husband was gone for the next three months for work. During that time, I realized just how unhappy I had been. I realized that I didn't care what people thought anymore. I knew I could do it on my own. I deserved happiness, and so did my children. They deserved to know what it was like to live in a home filled with peace, joy, and unconditional love. They deserved to laugh and have fun.

The time had come. It was time for me to reclaim my life, my independence, and most of all, to learn to love myself unconditionally. This book is a collection of stories and moments that chronicle my healing journey—the journey of healing my inner child, exploring my hopes and dreams, and reigniting my voice. It's a personal account of my path to rediscovering and loving the woman I was and the woman I am becoming.

Here's to that journey.

Chapter 1

Taking Back My Life

A person without freedom is like a plant
without sunshine. It has no way to grow.

—Lovetoknow.com Quotes

One winter evening, I found myself reflecting on how much things had changed over the past few months. My older son had just returned from his first semester of college, having excelled academically, and he asked if he could spend the night at a friend's house to celebrate. I saw no harm in it and gave my permission. However, not long after, I heard his stepdad undermine my decision and tell my son, with a few choice words, that he wasn't going anywhere.

What struck me in that moment was the realization that certain dynamics in my home were no longer in alignment with what I valued or what I was willing to accept for myself or my children. Coming after a period of relative peace, this episode felt like a turning point, and I knew that a decision had to be made. I encouraged my son to go ahead with his plans, and once he was gone, I finally faced a truth that had been building inside of me for a long time.

That night, I resolved to prioritize peace, independence, and self-respect. I had reached a point where I could no longer tolerate situations that made me, or my children, feel disrespected or mistreated. I made the decision to end a relationship that no longer served my well-being or aligned with my values. I wanted independence, freedom, and most of all, *peace*. I made a promise to myself that from this point forward, my main priority would be happiness for myself and my children. I wanted a divorce.

To my surprise, the next morning he got up and came along on a trip that was previously planned. He tried everything to reel me back in, but I went into full protective mode. I dug deep for all the strength and courage within me. I would no longer allow myself to stay in this situation. It was over. I had started to reclaim my life.

When we returned from the trip, I took time to gather my thoughts. I agreed to help during a period of recovery time for him after a surgery, but this only served to further strengthen my resolve. The emotional distance between us grew even wider, and I became more certain with each passing day that I was making the right decision.

Eventually, the conversation I had been dreading took place. I listened as reasons were laid out for why we should remain together, but none of them resonated with me. It became clear that we were no longer connected in the ways that mattered most to me—love, respect, core values, and understanding. At that moment, I realized that I had been living in a situation that did not truly see or support me as an individual.

In mid-January, the separation was finalized, and I felt an immense sense of relief. The energy in the house shifted, and for the first time in what felt like years, I could breathe freely. My children were understandably uncertain about what the future held, but I was confident that we had taken the first step toward healing. It was time to focus on recovery, forgiveness, and, most importantly, peace.

How do you start to heal? Where do you start? How do you find peace? I needed a trip to the beach—the one place where I could always connect with God and receive guidance, the one place I could feel at peace. The beach soothes my soul. I can sit for hours and just be in the moment with no stress.

As I write this chapter, I am sitting on a beach in Destin, Florida, totally inspired. It's been well over two years, and I feel totally connected with myself. I can sit here for hours and be present in the moment, knowing that Spirit is within me guiding me to love myself, love my boys, and love all that this life experience has to offer. I am at a place where I am living inspired and knowing that my *why* is about empowering and helping others.

My life experiences have led me to this exact place and moment for a reason. I believe that reason is so that I can serve others who have found themselves in similar experiences. It's about hope. It's about the journey of healing and becoming whole.

> In Japanese culture there is an art called kinsugi. When a fragile object is broken, they repair it with gold, and it increases the value of that object. Sometimes life breaks us into pieces. In such times repair yourself with golden qualities like self-love, compassion and patience. It will increase the value of your life.
>
> —@buddha_mindfulness_ on Instagram

Healing is about finding yourself, rediscovering your identity, learning to love yourself unconditionally, discovering your worth, embracing forgiveness, opening your heart, releasing anger and fear, and choosing love. Healing is about finding your inner confidence and listening to that inner voice that says *I can do anything I put my mind to*. Healing is about finding your freedom.

Courage, as defined by Oxford Languages Google, is the ability to do something that frightens you— strength in the face of pain or grief. It will take courage to look at yourself in the mirror and start doing the work. I assure you that you have that courage; it's waiting to roar.

Remember, healing doesn't happen overnight. You're in a marathon, not a sprint. I believe we each must find our path to true healing ourselves. I hope this book helps you repair the broken pieces with golden love so that you too will see your value.

This book is about my journey and what worked for me. If you can take one thing from it that will heal you, then my purpose is fulfilled. For me, it all started with saying *yes* to myself. I hope you chose to say *yes* to yourself. You deserve it. I see you.

The secret to happiness is freedom. The secret to freedom is courage. All your dreams can come true if you have the courage to pursue them.

—Corey Wadden

Chapter 2

Embracing the Waves of Grief: A Journey of Healing, Synchronicity, and Self-Discovery

Grief is like the ocean: it comes on waves ebbing and flowing. Sometimes the water is calm, and sometimes it's overwhelming. All we can do is learn to swim.

—Vicki Harrison

April 25th, 2022: I was five months into defining my identity and reclaiming my life. I had learned to laugh again, started to love myself, and was living my best life—or at least I thought I was. I was on my annual girls' beach trip when I got the call that would stop my soul. It stopped me in my tracks and pierced every part of me.

My sister Gabby had been in a horrible car accident and was being flown to a trauma center. I was two hours away, and I felt like I couldn't get there quick enough. The next five days were just a blur. On April 29, her soul left us. I felt like I couldn't breathe. There was a hole so deep and so painful—something I'd never experienced. How was I going to get through this? Why did this happen?

When I start reflecting, there were so many spiritual encounters that had taken place three weeks before the day of her accident—little things that just reminded me that I needed my faith, friends, and family. My friends had thrown me a fiftieth birthday party, and my other sister, Arristie, came to it. I was so thrilled to have her there with me. Over the years, my siblings and I had grown apart for various reasons. Later, I would find out that Gabby had insisted on Arristie coming to the party. (I am proud to say Arristie and I are now closer than I could have ever dreamed. She is my best friend.)

The morning of Gabby's accident, I was sitting on the beach when a woman had walked up to our group and started speaking to us. Now, if you know me, when I go to the beach, I tend to be somewhat of a recluse. While I may be in the group with all the ladies, I am usually reading a book and minding my own business. This is where I connect with Spirit, and everything else going on is completely blocked out. For some reason, I could feel this woman looking at me, and I was slightly nudged by something to look up at her.

She began sharing her story. She told us that she'd had a stroke. When she was in the hospital, the doctors were telling her husband that she wouldn't make it. She told us she was unable to speak but could hear everything that the doctors said.

Over the next few days of Gabby being in the hospital, I ran into this woman and her friends a few times. One of the days, they prayed with me, and she told me that it wasn't a coincidence that we'd met. God had directed her over that first morning to speak to me. She told me I needed to be Gabby's voice since Gabby couldn't speak.

Gabby held on for a few more days so that everyone was able to say goodbye. Then in Gabby's true fashion, she decided to go out on her own terms and donate her organs, saving five other human lives. Each of these moments was a *divine synchronicity*— things that were divinely guided for me to experience.

Losing Gabby taught me that one of the most selfless acts we can do as humans is to show unconditional love and help people who might not be able to help themselves. Gabby lives on in our memories, but she is present with me every day in spirit. She is my guardian angel, always guiding and protecting me. While grief can cause so many different emotions, I have been able to find peace.

Grief is different for every individual. They say that it gets easier with time. I'm not sure about that statement. For me, it's about seeing and feeling each sign that is presented to me—the breeze that came out of nowhere when I was writing this sentence; the white feather that blew up on my leg walking down the beach; the red cardinal chirping on the fence until I acknowledged it; the rainbow, butterfly, or in Gabby's case, a dragonfly.

A friend gave me a deck of inspirational cards after Gabby died. I began pulling out a couple of cards each morning. I could shuffle the cards and mix them up, and four out of five times, I would pull out the dragonfly card. After several weeks, I started researching the meaning of dragonflies.

Dragonflies are one of the only creatures that can go up, down, forward, and backward. They love being by the water. The dragonfly signifies transformation—letting go of the past and transforming into the beautiful creature you were meant to be. I now have a beautiful dragonfly tattoo to remind me to always be open to change. Embrace the transformation. This was a divine synchronicity.

I am still processing the grief; however, it is more about focusing on the lessons, the positives, and the memories. I choose to focus on the things that bring me peace. Yes, I have moments of sadness, but I choose not to loathe the sadness. I choose to celebrate the spirit that she is.

In losing Gabby, I realized something about grief. I had never grieved the various relationships and traumas that I had experienced. I was good at suppressing feelings, deleting them, and diving into my career. My career was my safe haven. It was the one place I felt safe, secure, confident, and valued. I discovered grief isn't always about the death of someone. Rather, it can be about letting a dream go, letting a friendship go, letting a relationship that does not serve your higher being go. It can be about letting go of a part of you that protected you all those years ago—releasing that inner hurt and loving that little child.

Going through grief and healing, I did the following things (remember, this is what worked for *me*):

- journaling
- Reiki
- meditation/yoga
- got Cooper, my fur baby, who loves unconditionally.
- grounding—getting outdoors daily
- reading—finding books of inspiration

- nutrition—eating things that made me feel good and would give me energy (Yes, food can fuel your mindset and emotions.)
- moving my body—daily workouts
- neuro-linguistic programming
- writing (Gabby's death led me to writing this book.)

We will dive into each of these things with the hope that it will empower you to see *you*.

In one of the books I read during this time (I can't remember which one it was), there was a concept that stuck with me: each person comes into our life for a reason. Some people will be a part of our life for a season and others for the whole time we're in this human experience. I see each relationship as an assignment from God. Either the person or situation is here to teach me something or I am here to teach them. Either way, seeing things from a different perspective—everything as a gift, even the bad things—has changed my outlook on life. I embrace each moment and do my best to show up with love and grace. I choose happiness and love every day. Yes, I have moments that are not all roses and sunshine, but I do not live in that moment.

The day Gabby left us, I went for a long run on the beach. I was in my own world and didn't realize the beach was empty and a storm was approaching. I was about two miles from my condo when the skies opened up and the downpour started. There was thunder and lightning all around me.

I was crying tears of pure grief when a light poured from the sky amidst the dark. It was a message: Look at the light to direct you through the darkness. You must go through the darkness to get to the light. *Sis, it's time you look into yourself and discover what you are passionate about. What sets your soul on fire? Go back to your passion. What are you great at? Take some time, pause and work on you. There's a beautiful soul within that just needs to show up for herself with unconditional love and grace.*

This message was what I needed to hear. I realized over the next year that not only would I grieve the loss of Gabby, I would grieve the loss of the past relationships. I would grieve the expectations, broken promises and dreams that had not come true. During this pause, I would let go of the grief and see each thing as a lesson. I would choose to see each event with love, releasing the anger, shame, guilt, and judgment. I would look deep within to see my role in each broken relationship. I would feel them, mourn them, and then look for the lesson. Finally, I would choose to forgive, release them, and move forward.

I started focusing on the message I received that day about looking within and finding my purpose. Now, as a consultant, I help people discover their purpose, their *why,* all the time. It was time for me to go to my *why*—my purpose.

Chapter 3

Look Within to Your Purpose

The purpose of life is to discover your
gift. The work of life is to develop it. The
meaning of life is to give your gift away.

—David Viscott

One of my fondest memories as a child was going to the beauty shop, the Foxy Lady, with my grandmother. I looked forward to these days because they filled my soul. As I opened the door to the salon, on the right side were probably twenty hooded dryers, all filled with ladies who had rollers in their hair. Manicure tables sat in front of them so they could get their nails done, and to the left were all of the styling chairs, with a stylist standing behind each one, talking and making people look and feel good.

I was always mesmerized by the owner of the salon, Miss Dee. She had this pitch-black Vidal Sassoon bob haircut, red nail polish, and black wing eyeliner with false lashes. *Glamourous* and *fabulous* was what she was. She was also kind and compassionate, and she empowered each person who came into her presence. She was so well put-together and always made people smile. Going to the salon was a confirmation that my purpose in life was to be a part of the beauty industry so that I could make people look good and feel good, as well as help them see their inner beauty like Miss Dee used to.

I have over thirty years in the beauty industry now, and it has always been both a humbling experience and a privilege to meet so many beautiful human beings. That hour to two hours with each person—customizing a look, listening, building relationships, making them feel seen, heard, and valued—would fill my soul like nothing else. It's crazy to think that as a small child, I knew my purpose in life was to empower people to see their inner beauty, to help them discover their own confidence and love themselves. Each one of us is worthy and valued, and no one can take that from us unless we let them.

Helping people see their worth and find their confidence has always been one of my strongest characteristics or abilities in life. It's my gift. What is crazy to think about is that somewhere along my personal journey, I forgot to do all those things for myself—the things that I teach others to do. I gave up control and lost who I was. What everyone saw was a strong person—put-together, confident, a leader, a successful business owner, a mom, and a great friend. What they didn't see was that I had a hard time looking at myself in the mirror and loving myself.

Learning to forgive myself for the things that took place in my life was tough—things such as molestation, sexual trauma, and mental and verbal abuse. I know and understand that these things are not my fault, but that does not change the feelings of guilt, shame, anger, and fear. I also now understand that a lot of these emotions and feelings served as a protection to myself to never be in that situation again.

I know that each life event, good and bad, has led me to a point where I can live out my purpose. These events have helped me develop empathy, compassion, resilience, forgiveness, and so much more. They have also led me to embrace my purpose: the purpose of serving others, coaching, and guiding people to find their self-worth.

I was meeting with my spiritual advisor recently, and she told me I was a natural healer. Part of my journey in this human experience is to help heal people. No, I'm not talking about healing an illness; I am talking about healing the inner being, the mind and the spirit. I know that I am supposed to help others on their journey of self-discovery, healing and finding their purpose or *why*. The best way for me to do that is to continuously work on and heal myself.

You may be asking, "How do I find my purpose? How do I discover my *why*? Who am I?" When you remove all the conditioned beliefs, opinions, and expectations of others, who are you? That's right: forget about what everyone says you are supposed to be and do and just listen to that inner voice saying *Who am I?*

One of the greatest things about awakening and starting over is freedom: the freedom to choose who you will become. You get this amazing opportunity to reinvent yourself, to become the best version of who you want to be. So now you get to ask yourself, do you want to be a loving, kind, and giving person, or do you want to be a sad, angry, resentful, and fearful person? Do you want to be someone who lives guarded with a shield up? Or do you want to live a life that is carefree and lived to the fullest? Do you want to live a life embracing your purpose and serving others? Do you want to laugh and embrace each moment that life has to offer?

When is the last time you really thought about who you are, who you want to be, and what that inner gut feeling is telling you your purpose is? It is time to get real, remove the beliefs that other people have placed upon you, and celebrate your independence. Let go of all those beliefs, excuses, and fears. Embrace and celebrate the human that you want to be. Embrace the purpose that you were put here to do.

Trust me, when you feel beaten and battered, it is hard to even think about the answers to these questions. However, I encourage you to dig deep and think about each one. Take some time to get silent and listen to that inner voice. Meditate and ask Spirit to give you the answers. Listen to your gut, which is Spirit/God telling you the answers. You don't have to have all the answers today. Give yourself some time to discover who you are. Rely on God to show you the way.

Here is a great exercise to do to find your *why*. Get outside in nature. Find a place where you can relax, get grounded, and connect with Spirit. Have a journal and a pen close by. Take some deep cleansing breaths. Clear your mind and open your heart. Ask Spirit/God, your angels, your spirit guides, spirit animals (whatever you personally believe in), to give you clarity and show you the answers.

Ask yourself the following questions:

- What sets my soul on fire?
- What brings me joy?
- What am I passionate about?
- What gets me out of bed every day?
- What do I love doing?
- What is my gut telling me to do?
- What is the greatest assignment that was placed on my heart, that feeling or desire that never leaves?
- Who am I?

Once you have meditated, grab your journal and freely write. Write whatever thoughts, feelings, and emotions come to play. Pour it all out on paper. You may need to do this multiple times, but silence is the key. You must quiet the world around you, quiet the voices of others, and listen to your gut.

I'm an avid reader and love books on leadership, communication, and growth. Over the last two years, I dove into self-help books, spiritual books, all things to help me live into my higher being. What I soon realized is that my biggest cheerleader had to be me. Your biggest cheerleader must be you as well.

In addition to owning a salon company and boutique, I work for an amazing consulting company. Heather Bagby, our vice president, often says, "Borrow our voice until you find yours." What I am saying to you is borrow my voice, my energy, my inner strength, my love, and my confidence until you find your own.

I have had the privilege of seeing Jamie Kern Lima, the

founder of IT Cosmetics, speak multiple times. She speaks so eloquently and is passionate about helping people see their worth and never give up on their dreams. Recently on an Instagram post, she talked about listening to that inner voice—that voice that keeps telling you to move forward and stay focused, even though the world around you is saying something else. Listen to that voice. It's your *why*.

> Know your why. Then fly girl fly.
>
> —Jamie Kern Lima

Once you know your *why*, listen to that inner voice and start pursuing your dreams. My life journey has brought me various careers, but the one thing that has stayed consistent is my *why*. What started out as being a hairstylist and wanting to make people feel good and have confidence led me to opening my own salon company to empower other hairstylists, guiding them to their inner confidence and showing them how to serve others while making an amazing living. I now have a group of shareholders and leaders in my salon company who are empowering others and living out their dream.

Becoming a consultant/coach is about passing the information that grew me as a leader and person, as well as grew my company, on to other salon owners and service providers, giving them the confidence and the know-how to lead a successful business while honoring themselves and their *why*. Team Leader is about empowering other coaches/consultants to see their value and worth as a coach and serve others.

Now I am writing a book about finding your inner voice,

healing, and having the confidence to live life to your highest self. This is my purpose. It is what sets my soul on fire and gets me out of bed every day: the purpose of serving others and leading them to their personal freedom, healing, dreams, and ultimately unconditional love. I see the potential in each person I meet. My wish is that each individual can see their own potential and go for it.

Your *why* may change, and that is OK too. The important thing is to listen to your intuition and act. When you listen to your *why* and start serving others, it is truly a magical healing experience.

As I pursued my *why*, I knew that I would need guidance and support. Therefore, I have surrounded myself with a powerful team of people who are there to hold me accountable, to challenge me, to cheer me on in becoming my higher self. They are my Power Team. My Power Team is my voice when I can't find mine. They are the people who I trust, I hold dear, and will hold me accountable to living out my purpose. They hold me to the highest standards with unconditional love.

I will tell you all about my Power Team and how each person on the team has helped me become who I am in a later chapter. For now, start thinking about what and who you need to be to fully experience your *why*.

Chapter 4

Finding My Confidence

Life is happening for us not to us.

—Tony Robbins

I am hell-bent on learning lessons and breaking patterns. I know that everything we do in life has a purpose and there's a reason that we go through it. I have been on a growth journey my entire life. After all the years I spent growing to be a great leader and a great mom, it was now time to take a dive into healing and finding myself—growing into the best version of myself.

The decision to dive into why I did the things I did was one that would open a whole new world for me—an awakening, a transformation, a spiritual journey, a journey to finding my inner peace, power, strength, and most of all, love for myself. It was time I started seeing me for *me*. This would require me to dive into all the emotions, feelings, lessons, and beliefs that I had been conditioned to accept. Let me be clear as I divulge these experiences: I do not see myself as a victim. I see myself as a victor! Each experience has made me the woman I am today. Finding my confidence as well as my voice has been a process.

Journaling is a daily activity that I've done for years, and it is a big part of my healing. I believe starting each day with gratitude is what kept my sanity and positivity all these years. Writing five things that I am grateful for each day set the mood for the day. I chose to get up every day and find something to be grateful for. The simple act of opening my eyes and breathing is a daily opportunity for gratitude.

Did you know that it's scientifically impossible to be in a state of gratitude and sadness/anger at the same time? The brain cannot do both. The practice of daily gratitude releases feel-good hormones—dopamine and serotonin. Imagine that you can set the mood each day just by writing down three to five things for which you are grateful.

With gratitude in mind, I needed to start looking at each day, event, people, moment, both good and traumatic, as a blessing. I know this is a unique perspective and not an easy one. Looking at the trauma and finding a positive can be a challenge. However, if you open your heart and meditate on it, you will find the positive. I now know that each experience has set me up for a greater purpose. I know without any doubt that my role on this earth is to influence people to find their inner strength, voice, and confidence.

I would not be able to relate to people if I hadn't personally gone through molestation, a narcissistic religion experience, a narcissistic relationship, and many other traumas. These events have led me to where I am today. Full disclosure: no one deserves to be molested, abused, raped, etc. No one asks for this and should ever have to experience it. However, it happens more than any of us would like to admit. Many of us do not want to talk about it; however, I am here to change that.

The healing journey has not been easy and is a daily process. There are days that are easier than others. The next few chapters will go over some of the techniques and therapies I have put in place to heal my inner soul.

Sexual abuse and trauma statistics are alarming and heartbreaking. As a society, we have to do better. It is believed that

- 1 in 3 girls have been sexually abused
- 1 in 5 boys have been sexually abused
- more than 80 percent of sexual abuse goes unreported
- more than 40 percent of young girls who have been molested experience sexual trauma and rape when they become an adult. The sad truth is that myself along with so many others are a part of this statistic.

Please know that I am grateful for each experience because it has taught me how to have empathy, grace, compassion, resilience, and unconditional love. Through my awakening, I have embraced the knowledge that each encounter is an assignment from GOD. We are supposed to learn something, or maybe we are supposed to teach someone something. With various therapies, I have been able to reassign a different meaning to the trauma.

One of the biggest lessons for me is to navigate life from a place of love versus fear. These experiences taught me what I would tolerate, and to love myself with grace and unconditional love. All of this led me to where I am right now, at this moment. It gave me the knowledge and the experience to author this book, as well as speak publicly about the events.

I learned to find hope and gratitude each day amongst the piles of shit. I learned to look at things from a different perspective. All of this has supported me in finding my inner voice as well as supporting my greater purpose in life: empowering others to love themselves, to find their inner strength and confidence.

Upon awakening, let the words THANK YOU flow
from your lips, for this will remind you to begin
your day with gratitude and compassion.
—Dr. Wayne Dyer

The second part of journaling is about exploring all my emotions—the good, bad, sad, happy, etc. A few years ago, my leadership coach, Jennifer Culverhouse, suggested I use a *feeling wheel* when journaling so that I could explore different emotions and thoughts. As I started this practice, I remember thinking to myself, *This isn't right. There's too many negative words on this wheel. I want to write about positive, happy things.* I told Jenn this in one of our sessions, and she replied, "There is no right or wrong when it comes to what we feel.

The words are just descriptions of different emotions. It does not make you weak to feel sadness, anger, or stress; it makes you human. It's OK to feel each of these things. You must be willing to explore each of these emotions so that you can heal."

This doesn't mean that we live in sadness, fear, anger, or grief. What it does mean is that instead of suppressing these emotions that don't feel good, we feel them, and then we let them go. It does not mean that you are weak; rather it shows your vulnerability and strength. I had been taught that showing these emotions was a sign of weakness. I now know that emotions are not that at all. As Jennifer Culverhouse says, "*Softness* is my greatest strength."

One of my mentors, Michael Cole, speaks of *top 20* and *bottom 80* behaviors. I took his philosophy and applied it to my thoughts. If I was going negative, angry, even sad, I acknowledged it. I gave myself a few minutes to explore the emotion, then I would look for the opposite—the positive. I would write it down, then let it go.

Letting something that you cannot control go is one of the most gratifying things you can do for yourself. Leaving a narcissist was about me letting go of something I could not control. I cannot control what anyone else does. However, I *can* control my reactions and my response. Learning this lesson is huge, and I am still a work in progress.

Journaling is about loving yourself. It is about having an outlet to express and explore all the thoughts, disappointments, dreams, hopes, emotions, and goals that are right within you. Journaling is renewing to the soul. There is no right or wrong in what you feel or write. It is about learning to see things as they are and showing up with unconditional love.

I am currently enrolled in a class for my neuro-linguistic programming certification, and we are studying cognitive journaling. The class emphasizes that journaling will help you become aware of your thought patterns and emotional tendencies. Journaling will allow you to disrupt these patterns. Awareness is key.

> What you are aware of you can control,
> what you are unaware of will control you.
>
> —Michael Cole

The following are some tips for journaling:

- **Find a quiet space to be present.** I love the outdoors.
- **Use a notebook or journal.** There are many different types of journals available, from gratitude journals to day-planners. I have used all of them. Now I use a beautiful blank journal or notebook with a beautiful cover. I like to find journals that have meaning in the moment. Currently I am using a journal with a dragonfly on it. The dragonfly has meaning in my life and reminds me that every day, I am transforming.
- **Write with different-colored ink pens.** I love using different colors to show shifts in thought. They also allow me to see moods and patterns based on the color of ink I chose.

- **Meditate.** Ask God to let the words flow freely, then write.
- **Don't judge.** You cannot judge yourself for your thoughts. Show those thoughts and that part of yourself unconditional love.

The more I journal, the freer I feel. Journaling has allowed me to have a voice, especially when I've felt that my voice didn't matter. Journaling is a powerful tool that has helped me dig deep within to find my strength. I truly believe that gratitude journaling is what kept me going through all the years of trauma. I always had that inner voice saying, *You are good enough. Don't let him take that from you.*

I have learned that no one can take something from you unless you give it to them. Do not give anyone that power. Journaling is about me having an outlet. It's about me taking my power back, finding my voice and confidence.

Chapter 5

Unconditional Love Starts with Loving Yourself

Unconditional love, simply put, is love without
strings attached.
It's love you offer freely. You don't base it on what
someone does for you in return.
You simply love them and want nothing
more than their happiness.

—Crystal Raypole

Unconditional love doesn't mean remaining in a situation that harms you, whether physically or emotionally. It's about releasing hate, resentment, and judgment—toward both others and yourself. I'm a work in progress, but each day I strive to show up for myself with grace, understanding, and compassion for who I was, who I am, and who I am becoming. That's the essence of unconditional love.

Now, imagine offering yourself the same love you so freely

give to others. Or better yet, what if you loved yourself in the way you've always desired to be loved?

How do you love yourself? This chapter is dedicated to the things you can do to love yourself. Let me be clear that loving yourself is not selfish—it is selfless! Let us explore the many things you can do to love yourself.

Solitude

Solitude isn't something people connect to self-love. However, after leaving a relationship, it is so important to take some time to reconnect and find yourself. I realize looking back that after each relationship, I dove into another relationship within a month or even weeks. I found myself looking to fill the loneliness with someone else, never giving myself time to heal. I didn't take time to learn from the lessons and truly find myself. I was looking for outside validation.

The book *Eight Rules of Love* by Jay Shetty has an entire chapter devoted to "Let Yourself Be Alone." He states, "Loneliness makes us rush into relationships: it keeps us in the wrong relationships: and it urges us to accept less than we deserve."

How does being alone feel? Why is it uncomfortable? Can you go sit at a restaurant and have a meal by yourself? Can you go to a museum or movie by yourself? There is nothing wrong with being alone. However, society spends so much time pressuring us to have a relationship, have kids, be a part of something. While there is nothing wrong with any of those things, what *is* wrong is not being comfortable with who you are. Solitude is necessary for you to truly connect with who you are, what you want, and what you need versus what everyone else says you need.

I have learned to schedule alone time with no distractions—time to be present with myself. For me, I love being alone outside on my patio, at the beach, or even in a park, any quiet place where I can be present with my thoughts and soak in life. This is time where I learn about myself as well as my wants and needs. Sometimes in this solitude I journal, read, meditate, or just sit peacefully in gratitude for this amazing life.

One of my favorite clients, Miss Marilyn, who just turned one hundred years old this past December, loves being alone. She grew up in an era where if you weren't married by twenty, you were an *old maid*. We laugh about that, because she has more spunk and joy than anyone I know.

Miss Marilyn turned eighteen the day that Pearl Harbor was bombed, so in her words, "all the eligible bachelors had gone to war." Up until the last few years, Miss Marilyn would travel all over the US. Every week, we would discuss her adventures and how much she loved seeing the world, experiencing everything imaginable. Miss Marilyn knows who she is, and what she will accept and not accept. She lives by her core values and will never settle for anything less.

Do you know what you want? Do you know what your core values are? What are your nonnegotiables? The answers to these questions will only come with a deep dive into yourself. You need to shush the outside voices and maybe even the inside voices for a while to truly get grounded in what you want and deserve.

Learn to be present with yourself. Love for yourself. Learn how things make you feel. Prioritize yourself and the things that make you feel joy, love, and happiness. Once you truly learn yourself, you will learn to respect yourself, your wants and your needs. This is unconditional love in its purest form. Jay Shetty recommends in his book to take some time learning a new skill, hobby, or trade. Do something for *you*. What I have personally learned is that the more I challenge myself to learn something new, the more I grow. It allows my creativity to soar. My confidence grows as I spread my wings to fly.

Writing a book has been a big challenge. It meant taking time for myself to dive into all the *stuff*—the things we do not want to talk about or feel. It meant learning how to do something that was uncomfortable. I knew absolutely nothing about writing a book. However, taking time for myself to discover this new skill led to increased knowledge and confidence.

I enrolled in various classes on writing until I found the one that spoke to me. It has been an amazing learning experience. I challenge you to spend some time transitioning from being lonely to being fully present with yourself to explore and love all of you. Take up a new skill, hobby, or language. Learn to grow yourself.

With growth comes change and
with change comes growth.
—Unknown

Physical Movement

I learned a long time ago that to be mentally healthy and strong, I had to be physically strong. I adjusted my diet and workout plans and started making changes in my daily routine. I started researching foods and playing around with what I ate.

Before my third marriage, I ate clean. However, he did not like the house to smell like food, so eating out was an everyday event. Slowly but surely, I let go of control and caved in to the rules and regulations. My health was severely affected. I developed acid reflux to the point that I would involuntarily vomit. I started having chest pains. I could not even do a minute on a treadmill.

After a year of tests and doctors' visits, I ended up in Rochester, Minnesota, at the Mayo Clinic. The doctor told me I had the heart of an eighty-year-old woman; I was only forty-five. The only cure was to do daily exercise. For the first time in a long time, I was excited. I was eager to get back to the gym and start taking care of *me* again.

That night, after leaving the doctor's office, I remember sitting at dinner with my then-husband. As I picked up my phone to text a friend who owned a gym, letting him know I planned to return on Monday, my husband told me, "No need to do that. I've already ordered weights and a treadmill for you. I know going back to the gym might be hard, especially since you're out of shape and your schedule doesn't really allow time for the gym."

In that moment, my excitement faded. I began working out at home every day, but the feelings of shame and guilt for "letting myself go" weighed heavily on me. Looking back, I now understand that this was a subtle form of control. I don't think he was even fully aware of what he was doing, but his own insecurities were being projected onto me, and I unknowingly allowed it. It wasn't right, and it felt hurtful, but it was a reflection of his struggles, not my worth.

After the divorce, a friend suggested I go back to the gym, since I had hit a plateau with my at-home workouts. For whatever reason, I had a mental block around the gym. I went to a local gym, and for the first time in my life, I felt anxiety, like a panic attack. Once I left the gym, I sat in the car crying and could barely breathe. What the hell was going on with my body?

That afternoon, I had a call with my life coach, and we worked through it. Little did I realize the event from so many years before with my ex, that one statement that I was overweight and self-conscious, had me in full panic protection mode. I didn't want others to judge me. I felt ashamed and embarrassed. Hell, *I* was judging me!

My life coach helped walk me through an exercise to release this belief and replace it with a positive anchor. Basically, I went back to the days when I was a gym rat. My confidence was strong. I felt healthy, had lots of energy, and looked great. This became my motivation for who I was becoming. I anchored these feelings deep within to get to where I wanted to be. I put a picture up on my mirror that I saw daily that would remind me of who I wanted to be. This picture anchored the mind-set I needed to be the best version of me.

The next day, I walked into a different gym and found my

personal trainer, Joe Robertson. Joe is part of my Power Team. He is truly an amazing human being and knows exactly how to push me to become the best version of myself. The workouts are not just physical but mental as well. They are therapeutic. Joe has a way of connecting the workouts to the mind-set. When a strong positive emotion is connected to the work, it no longer seems impossible.

Each day with my new workouts I got physically and mentally stronger. The benefits of this part of my journey were amazing and included the following:

- I started believing in myself again.
- My self-confidence grew stronger day by day.

- I started shedding the weight, but more importantly, I started shedding the BS I had been conditioned to believe.
- My self-esteem and self-confidence were reappearing.
- My energy levels were back at their peak.
- My physical strength and mental strength were now at their peak.

No one deserves to feel unworthy and unloved. People do not always connect physical workouts with mental healing, but they go hand in hand. Moving your body stimulates the production of endorphins—chemicals in the brain that function as natural painkillers and mood elevators. The endorphins reduce feelings of anxiety, stress, and depression. Exercise also lowers levels of the stress hormone cortisol.

The best thing you can do for your mind, body, and spirit is to move your body daily. If something isn't working, find someone who can guide you. There are so many health plans, books, and diets. You must find what will work for you.

My belief is that moving for a minimum of thirty minutes a day will give my body what it needs to perform at its peak. The days when I work out with Joe, I move for an hour or more. Physical movement and food go hand in hand. They will support each other. If you are not able to hire a personal trainer or a nutritionist, investigate the various books that are out there and find one that will work for you.

I do not personally believe in dieting; to me, that is a setup for failure. What I believe in is a healthy lifestyle—behaviors and habits that will give my body everything it needs.

Healthy Lifestyle

In addition to working out, the boys and I embarked on a health journey that included healthy food. We have all heard of the benefits of eating veggies, fruit, and fish, and drinking plenty of water. However, this is difficult for many people. As I've studied more about food, I've found that some people eat for comfort, some for socializing, and some for survival.

I love food and socializing, and sometimes I do go to food for comfort. Coca-Cola was my vice for many years. I ran on sugar and caffeine. I have now reprogrammed my brain to choose foods that support my mind, body, and spirit. I fill my body with foods that will enhance each area of my body: energy, nutrition, and functionality. I focus on foods that will help me become the best version of *me* for everyone around me, as well as and most importantly myself.

My goal is to avoid processed foods, preservatives, sugars, dairy, hormones, and all the other stuff that is not pure. Our bodies cannot process these things. Through my research, it is clear that the more stuff you put in your body that is not living and coming from the earth, the more ailments, illnesses, and lack of energy you will experience. I travel multiple times a month, so I must have a plan in place to support my success. I travel with healthy snacks so that I'm not tempted to go to sugar and processed foods. I replaced the candy with fresh veggies, fruit, and nuts. I look for healthy restaurants near me. If I am in one location for several days, I will order groceries and snacks that are good for me versus heading to the restaurants.

Our bodies were made to support our well-being. However, with fast-paced living and an easy grab-and-go mentality, we have destroyed that greatness. It is up to you to start taking care of yourself. Show yourself love by giving your body what it needs and what it can process.

My love for cooking has been reignited. Meal prepping is now a part of our regular routine. A major change in mindset was key. I now see my body as a gift from God, and it is my responsibility to love and take care of it. Feeding my body only good things gives me more energy, makes me feel better and look better, and most of all, has restored my confidence and love. Eliminating the foods that are not good for you is a lifestyle change worth pursuing.

Growing up, I remember Dad always having a garden, and he still does to this day. Fresh veggies were always a part of our meals. (Full disclosure: they were not cooked in a healthy way, but that is for another book lol.) With this thought in mind, I started a small box garden with a few veggies a couple of years ago. That garden has now grown into multiple boxes with lots of vegetables, herbs, and plants.

What started as a hobby to grow my own vegetables and know that they were healthy turned into another healing venture: growing and keeping something alive as well as getting grounded by caring for something. This is very therapeutic. Starting from seeds and growing them into a plant has been fascinating. Watching the veggies grow and having good clean food for the boys and me is a win. I recently grew my first watermelon plant. It was so good. My family and friends laughed at me when they came to visit, as I would have to show them "all of my baby watermelons."

In addition to loving yourself through the foods that you eat, gardening has many other benefits, including the following:

- exercise (digging, planting, weeding)
- sunlight and its natural Vitamin D, which aids in bone health, immune building, and energy
- stress relief—therapeutic and relaxing, a great way to get grounded and relax
- sense of accomplishment and confidence as you nurture and care for something

Watching plants grow is satisfying. Learning to care for and nurture each plant is like nurturing your very soul. You must figure out exactly what you need to grow and prosper. Remember, sometimes we must adjust the water intake, add fertilizer, or move locations to get better sunlight. The same needs apply to us as humans. Sometimes we need to adjust our environment and change our diets, workout routines, or even the people we hang out with to truly grow and thrive.

The following are some terrific books on health and nutrition:

- *Living Good Daily* by Dr. Livingood
- *Grit and Grace: Train the Mind Train the Body, Own Your Life* by Tim McGraw
- *Body Love: Live in Balance, Weigh What You Want, and Free Yourself from Drama Forever* by Kelly Leveque

Pampering Yourself

Taking time for yourself may be one of the most challenging things to do. I know life is busy, especially if you are a mom, worker, caregiver, entrepreneur, whatever the case may be. I understand carving time for yourself is difficult. I call this time *white space*—or rather, my leadership coach, Jennifer Culverhouse, calls it that.

In one of my sessions with her, she encouraged me to start putting white space on my calendar. This time was dedicated to me. There could not be anything in that time block. I realized how much I had missed this. Prior to owning a business, marriage, and becoming a mom, I used to get a massage every other week (I know, extreme—however, it was great for me). I still would get massages and other things when I felt like I was at the breaking point, but that was not being proactive.

I sat in a class with Rachel Hollis, and she described a vase full of water. As you start watering all the things around you—family, friends, partner, work, etc.—and keep pouring into everyone else, the vase will eventually run out. However, if you fill your vase with all the stuff—sleep, love, food, exercise, pampering yourself, growth, etc.—the vase will get full, and the water will overflow onto everyone around you. You cannot pour from an empty cup (vase).

White space, or time for yourself, is crucial for your mental health and well-being, just as much as it is for everyone around you. We have all heard the announcement on an airplane to "put your oxygen mask on first" before helping another. Well, it's time to start healing yourself and put your oxygen mask on first.

The following are good ways to pamper yourself:

- bubble baths
- massages
- manicures/pedicures
- facials
- taking a walk
- meditation
- six to eight hours of sleep
- shopping
- reading a book
- breath work

Taking some time to relax, release, and allow someone to pamper you is an act of self-love. Go ahead: make your white space and get some TLC. Schedule something that is good for you.

> If your compassion does not include
> yourself, it is incomplete.
> —Jack Kornfield

Nature

Nature is a natural healer. It provides you with everything you need to fill your heart, soul, mind, and body. It gives you a place to connect with Spirit and get grounded. It is a space to see yourself as the beautiful creation of God that you are. Seeing all the beautiful things that were created for you helps you see just how special a creature you are.

Nature is my space to relax, release, and breathe in the goodness. It provides me with peace—peace like no other. The stillness is breathtaking. I am sitting outside while I write this chapter, and I can feel the words flowing freely to the page. There's a cool breeze, the sun is shining, and the skies are clear. A butterfly has been flying around all morning, along with a baby dragonfly. A red cardinal appears from time to time and chirps.

When you quiet your mind and sit in nature, it is amazing all the things you notice. Nature calms the soul and helps you lift your vibrational frequency. Have you ever been upset and decided to take a walk to calm down and get clarity? That is nature at work. That is connecting with your higher self and allowing God to direct you back to love. Nature is a healer.

Everyone likes something different when it comes to nature. You may prefer the lake, the woods, the mountains, or the beach. Being in nature gives your body a break from the electromagnetic pollution of electronic devices and the negative energy fields that surround us every day in the fast-paced society we live in. Nature allows your body to realign and balance itself. Taking time to be near water will elevate your mood and increase your serotonin levels. Nature is a great way to enhance mindfulness and presence.

Just as with the changing seasons, different people find beauty in various aspects of nature. Some may see winter as refreshing, with its cold air and magical snow, while others find peace and joy in the warmth of summer. Spring brings the fresh bloom of flowers, and fall offers the vibrant transformation of leaves. The rich tapestry of colors in autumn reflects the diversity and uniqueness of each person. Regardless of your preference for a particular season or natural setting, every part of nature provides its own form of healing.

I recently visited the Redwoods in California for the first time. I stood surrounded by these towering wonders and felt a complete sense of healing that words can't quite capture. Laughing, hugging trees, and just soaking in the beauty of these giants reminded me that I am resilient and that there is resilience in each one of us. Just like these trees, we can endure, stand tall, and grow through the toughest of times.

Where is your place to go? Where do you feel completely relaxed and grounded, the place where you feel connected to spirit? For me, it is the beach. If I can't get to the beach, I find a pool or a lake. I love spring, summer, and fall. The perfect seventy-five to eighty degrees of sunshine makes me happy. While winter is not my favorite season I can still find beauty in it. The point here is to get outside regularly and connect with God. Release and let your soul be filled with the pure joy of living life and being a fabulous human being.

Sleep

Sleep can be a powerful aid in healing ourselves. Most people need between seven and nine hours of sleep; however, I know some very happy successful people who operate on five. You must figure out what your body needs and then do it. A rested body leads to a rested mind.

Quality sleep helps with the following:

- restoration and repair of the body and mind
- building of the immune system.
- managing stress
- enhancing resilience

- clarity
- energy
- enhancing mood

The list goes on and on. When you're going through stuff, it's easy to crawl in bed and not want to get up, but that doesn't serve you or anyone around you. Listen to your body when it comes to sleep, but do not overdo it. Too much sleep can feed depression and anxiety, lower your energy, and more.

Reading

At one time, reading was my escape from reality. I would read love stories, trash novels, and fantasies, and drift away into another world. It was a great escape from reality. As I became an entrepreneur, I started gravitating toward leadership books, and hospitality and life-improvement books. The last couple of years, I have been diving into self-help (healing) books, as well as books on behavior and communication.

Reading provides me with the knowledge I need to grow and change. If there is something I want to do or become, I will read and study all of the things to become that. We are fortunate to be able to find people who have been successful in whatever arena we want to play in and learn from their mistakes and successes.

In my healing journey, I gravitate toward books that have guides, workbooks, and action items to do. I believe you can read or listen to as much as you want and yes, it will give you knowledge, but if you do not act, then everything stays the same. Many people say knowledge is power. I believe it's the taking action through that knowledge that is the true power.

If you're not a reader, then no worries. You can listen to books on audio or podcasts on various topics. Personally, I love to have a physical copy of a book. Part of my daily routine is reading for at least ten minutes. Some days I will read for hours. Reading is a relaxing tool for me.

Books on healing and finding your self-worth are numerous. I encourage you to find an author who speaks to your soul, pick up a book, and dive in. The right book always has a way of finding itself in your hands.

Several months ago, I was at an event and picked up several books by Dr. Wayne Dyer. Those books have sat on my shelf until recently. I was cleaning, and the book *Excuses Begone* fell on the floor. I picked it up and before I put it back on the shelf, I started to read the page it opened to. Sure enough, it was the message I needed to hear at that moment.

The following are some of my favorite books:

- *You Can Heal Your Life* by Louis Hay
- *Rising Strong* by Brené Brown
- *The Untethered Soul* by Michael A. Singer
- *Happy Days* by Gabrielle Bernstein
- *Eight Rules of Love* by Jay Shetty

Meditation

Meditation started out as a big challenge for me. It was suggested by my leadership coach to slow me down, but turning my brain off was not an easy task. I learned quickly that meditation wasn't about shutting the brain down; it was about letting thoughts surface or pass through. I didn't have to solve anything. I just needed to sit in silence and listen to that inner being.

I started off slowly with the focus of deep breathing. I found various meditations online that supported my goal of finding peace within. I often sleep with guided meditations; they help me relax and go to a beautiful place of peace while I sleep. Meditation and deep breathing have numerous benefits, starting with increasing the oxygen to your cells, which in turn gives you more energy. Meditation is known to help lower blood pressure, reduce stress, boost concentration, and more.

For me, meditation has become a form of therapy. It's a time where I can feel completely connected to God. The silence allows me to truly hear that inner guidance showing me the way. It's peace within myself. Taking time daily to sit and be present with no distractions is one of the most selfless acts you can ever do for yourself. The silence is healing to the soul.

One of my favorite guided meditations is "The Beach" by Colette Baron-Reid. Colette takes you on an eleven-minute guided meditation to let the chaos of the world go. You imagine yourself on a beach with the sun's warm glow, your body being flooded with a golden healing light. The soft voice of Colette will guide you through the process of breathing and letting things go. Meditation is a great way to connect the mind, body, and spirit, which we all know leads to great health.

Joy

Finding joy in life is a vital part of self-love. Joy is more than just a fleeting emotion; it's a deep sense of happiness, pleasure, and fulfillment. It can be experienced through a variety of activities, memories, and connections. What brings you joy? Perhaps it's dancing, singing, gardening, socializing, reading, cooking, exercising, painting, writing, or getting a massage.

Before my last marriage, my home was always a hub of activity. Family and friends gathered regularly for weekend cookouts, BBQs, crawfish boils, and pool parties. My door was always open, and my son's friends, along with our extended family and friends, were constant visitors. It wasn't until I lost this that I realized how much I had taken it for granted. But now, those gatherings are back, and my home is once again filled with the sound of laughter, the smell of food cooking, and the sight of everyone enjoying each other's company.

This simple, everyday joy is what I cherish most. My home is a revolving door of love, with friends and family coming in and out all day. My sister jokes that my front door is like a twenty-four-hour Walgreens—always open, and if by chance it's locked, everyone has the code to get in.

Today, I'm proud to say I've returned to the things that bring me joy, with one key difference: I've learned to set boundaries. If something doesn't bring me joy, it's a hard *no*. I no longer say *yes* out of obligation or guilt. Setting boundaries can be difficult, but they're essential for protecting your peace and avoiding unnecessary misery. Life is too short to spend even a moment being unhappy. We're not promised tomorrow, so living each moment with joy and purpose is the best way to honor your higher self.

Think of a young child—carefree, smiling, and without a worry in the world. As adults, we lose that sense of freedom, becoming consumed with what others think or say about us. I challenge you to reconnect with that inner child. Blow bubbles, play in the rain, dance like no one is watching. Embrace the moment and create your own joy.

I recently went to my niece's birthday party; it was at a roller rink. It brought back so many wonderful fun memories from my childhood. After the party, I purchased a pair of pink roller skates with neon lights. I now roller-skate on my back patio with old-school music playing. It is pure childlike fun for me.

Have you ever met a person who just lives life carefree, with no worries in the world? They don't care what people say or think. They live life on their terms. I had the privilege of connecting with an old friend from school, and that is exactly how he is. No worries in the world. He is silly, carefree, and doesn't give a fuck what anyone thinks. He reminded me that I was "Jennifer *fucking* Boutwell." It was time to let that inner child out, embrace life, and live it full of joy. Who cares what other people may think or say? They are not God, and their opinion is not our concern. Why should you stop living life to its fullest to accommodate someone else's expectations?

I will forever be grateful for that advice. Give yourself permission to live a life filled with joy. It's time to honor your greatness and love yourself. Experience joy and happiness on a different level. Go have fun and be childlike. Laughter and fun are truly the best medicine.

Puppy Love

Over the years, I always had dogs and cats. In the last divorce, I lost my dog. The fear of losing another puppy kept me from getting one. However, my sister had a different plan. In July of 2023, she surprised me with the most amazing present ever: a cute white Malti-shipoo named Cooper. Now this was love at first sight. There is no love like the love of a puppy.

Cooper is the most chill animal I've ever had. He sits and meditates with me every morning. He has taught me unconditional love. I come home, and he is sitting at the window waiting for me. Not a moment goes by that he's not near me. He gives meaning to the saying, "A dog is a man's best friend." While I was reluctant to have this responsibility, I am so grateful for this gift.

Chapter 6

Letting Go of Limiting Beliefs and Affirming the Life of Your Dreams

It's imperative to our healing journey that
we allow ourselves to be truly seen by first
seeing ourselves and loving ourselves.

—Gabrielle Bernstein, *Happy Days*

For years, I yearned for a loving, happy, and peaceful relationship, not realizing that the foundation of any healthy relationship begins within myself. The journey toward self-love, embracing all of me unconditionally, is now my greatest pursuit. To others, I appeared confident, but beneath the surface, I struggled with feelings of unworthiness and shame, and the belief that I didn't deserve the best life had to offer. This inner turmoil created a deep loneliness, but through my own journey, I've come to understand that many people share these same feelings.

After years of soul-searching, meditation, and Neuro-Linguistic Programming (NLP), I uncovered the conditioned beliefs that led me to feel inadequate. Repeated rejection and strict societal expectations only reinforced these beliefs. As a child, I was raised in a religion that was extremely rigid and judgmental, where everything was black and white, right or wrong, because "they" said so.

One pivotal moment occurred when I began dating outside my religious community. I found a large brown envelope in the hatchback of my car, with words cut out and glued onto it: "JENNIFER BOUTWELL HOW COULD YOU?" Inside were dozens of articles from the religious organization condemning me as a sinner and claiming that the devil had infiltrated my mind. There was also a detailed letter, composed of words cut from magazines and glued onto paper, telling me how horrible I was—that God didn't love me, that I was killing my mother. The accusations went on and on.

I was devastated and frightened. The fact that someone would go to such lengths to deliver this message, breaking into my car to do so, was mind-boggling. This person, who claimed to live by God's law, had broken all the rules to shame me, yet labeled me *worldly*.

Leaving that religious organization only intensified my isolation. Lifelong friends turned away, and I was treated as though I no longer existed. Although I was never officially excommunicated, I was effectively shunned. People would see me in public and refuse to speak to me. I was no longer invited to events and was marked as an outsider.

Several years passed, and I returned to the church for a special event, only to be met by one of the heads of the church. He abruptly stopped me from sitting down and told me that he would not allow me to corrupt any of "his" members. He informed me that he "knew about me," and I was not welcome. I was in my early twenties and remember being so angry, embarrassed, and ashamed. After telling him that he could go fuck himself, I walked out. This experience ingrained in me the belief that people would ultimately betray me, even people who were supposed to represent God.

As a child, I knew that I wanted to be a hairstylist. Each year of high school started with a meeting with the guidance counselor to discuss my future and what I wanted to become. I was an honor student making great grades according to society. My desire be a hairstylist did not sit well with the counselor. At each meeting, she would express her opinions: "Cosmetology is for stupid people. Cosmetology is for people who can't make it in college. Cosmetology is no way to make a living. You will be poor for the rest of your life." I would leave these meetings questioning my inner knowing.

Thank God the universe guided me to follow my gut and become a cosmetologist. However, for the first twelve years in the industry, deep down these statements would haunt me. I would find myself questioning my worth.

When you are taught that you are terrible for choosing to question or have a different belief system, it crushes your confidence, value, worthiness, and love. You start believing those thoughts about yourself, and you start living out that very scenario. That inner thought becomes your reality. I will say that while these beliefs affected a lot of what I did, I always seemed to know that there was more. I always had a knowing.

To make up for the lack of not being enough as a wife, mother, daughter, sibling, and friend, I chose to dive into work.

The more I worked, the more I felt needed and validated. The various things that had been said to me by people as well as society became my inner fuel to work harder and be *more*.

As my last marriage became my worst, I ran—straight to work. Success gave me what I thought I needed. The problem was that at some point, I would have to go home. Soon I realized that no matter how successful I was, it was not enough; it would never give me the love, acceptance, validation, and happiness that I wanted and needed. Work would not give me what I was looking for, only a temporary feeling of validation and worthiness. It also brought mom guilt, shame, and *you aren't there for your family* emotions. It was a double-edged sword. I needed to pause and evaluate where I was going and what I was doing.

While I tried to find myself, the feelings of guilt, shame, and judgment were in full affect. I was judging myself for not living up to the expectations that defined a good loving person, a good mother, friend, boss, and partner. Where did these beliefs come from? What determines right and wrong? What *is* right and wrong? Who are we supposed to listen to: family, society, news media, friends? I am not blaming any of my actions on these events. At the end of the day, everything I did was a choice—a choice that has led me to exactly where I am supposed to be.

I had the privilege of experiencing a brief segment on NLP at a Tony Robbins event, "Unleash the Power Within." That segment was the start of me seeing things from a different perspective. I decided to dive in and go through a full day of NLP with my brother-in-law, who is certified in NLP. This decision changed my life and did more for me in one day than the years of working with a therapist. (I am not saying that seeing a therapist is not good; what I am saying is that for me, NLP was the therapy that worked and helped me regain my identity.)

The first step in NLP was seeing my conditioned, limiting beliefs and patterns. We created a detailed timeline starting with first memories, happy memories, successes, and traumas, and placed them on the timeline. My brother-in-law has walls with whiteboards, and we filled every space with events, thoughts, statements, and moments. Seeing how each of these played out in each area of my life was like watching a movie. It was a long hard look in the mirror.

Fully understanding why I believed or thought something was so clear—where the thoughts came from, who they came from, and how they came to life. Clarity! Here's the big one: understanding and realizing how I had subconsciously viewed my worth, value, and lack of self-love. I now understood why I had chosen the relationships that I had. I understood why I would attack and fight back (all a protective mechanism).

We often hear people say *fight or flight*. I was the fighter. One of my beliefs was that fighting was the only way to not show weakness. Growing up as the only girl in the family for nine years, I had to fight or I was weak. You did not cry around the boys, because that just meant weakness. NLP gave me the means to see things as they were versus the story I had told myself for years.

The realization that I could love myself based on my own belief system was freeing and healing. Don't get me wrong— changing one's mind-set isn't easy. However, daily habits help. Seeing the timeline of events in my life written out on a whiteboard was an eye-opening experience. I could see when and how each conditioned, limiting belief was developed and where it came from.

For example, I believed that I could never trust a man, or anyone for that matter, because they would lie, cheat, steal, and eventually betray me. Hence the many broken relationships. This may sound silly, but I know so many people who have this same belief system. It comes from things that happen to us, and things we are told, see, and hear as children. I can't blame the people who taught me these beliefs, because they were taught the same by their parents, and them from their parents, and so on and on.

When you believe these things subconsciously, that is exactly what you will attract. How do you recognize and break these patterns, disrupt these beliefs? Awareness is crucial for moving forward. After NLP, I committed to being aware of my patterns and willing to disrupt them.

Another part of this type of therapy is something I learned from Tony Robbins. He teaches the six basic human needs: significance, certainty, uncertainty, love/connection, growth, and contribution. We all have these within us. When our main needs are not being met, we must do something different. I realized what needs were not being met within myself. I learned which human needs, if not met, would send me into a tailspin. I saw what I needed to work on.

While NLP does not break the patterns, it does have the capability to make a person aware. One of my mentors, Michael Cole, says, "What you see, you can manage; what you can't see manages you." NLP has given me the means to be aware of and recognize when I am running a pattern. The more aware I am, the more I can disrupt the pattern.

After you disrupt a pattern over and over, you eventually break the habit. Yes, I referred to it as a *habit*. When you do the same thing over and over, it is referred to as a habit. We all know and understand that not all habits are good. Therefore, it is important to become aware of the patterns that do not serve you in becoming your higher self.

One of my favorite books, *Excuses Begone: How to Change Lifelong, Self-Defeating Thinking Habits* by Dr. Wayne Dyer, breaks down the most common excuses—*mind viruses*, as he refers to them. The book is a great guide to seeing beliefs (excuses, mind viruses) and coming up with ways to disrupt them. This book teaches you how to convert an excuse into a positive affirmation. My favorite part is the paradigm of asking yourself seven simple questions. In the book, he breaks the top excuses down as well as going into depth on each paradigm question. Here is a summation of the paradigm:

1. *Is it true?* Probably not.
2. *Where did the excuses come from?* I allowed them.
3. *What is the payoff?* I get to avoid risk and stay the same.
4. *What would my life look like if I couldn't use these excuses?* I'd be free to be myself.
5. *Can I create a rational reason to change?* Easily.
6. *Can I access universal cooperation in shedding old habits?* Yes, by simply align him with my source of being.
7. *How can I continuously reinforce this new way of being?* I've been vigilant.

Once you become aware of the excuses and habits that no longer serve you, you can start changing and becoming the person you were created to be. After a year of living my life seeing and being aware of patterns and beliefs and disrupting them, I am proud to say I am enrolled in a class to get my certification in NLP. Becoming a certified practitioner is the next step in living into my purpose, empowering others to let go of the beliefs that are holding them back from living an extraordinary life.

NLP has been a huge part of my healing as well as my spiritual growth. Awareness and disruption of patterns is important, but you also must reprogram your thinking with positive thinking. This led me to daily affirmations and manifestations.

Affirmations

My director and I were walking through the Dallas Market shopping for boutique items. We came across a beautiful woman who stopped us at one of the booths and said she had a gift for us. It was this cool wraparound bracelet, and as she grabbed my hand and started to wrap this long leather strip around my wrist, she started saying words: *you are beautiful, you are enough, you are kind, you are awesome, you are amazing,* and so on. It was almost like a ritual as she steadily wrapped the leather strap around my wrist. I stood there in awe, as all I could think was *Man, do I need to hear these words.* A stranger just said everything I longed to hear.

When we are in the midst of chaos, trauma, and life,

we often forget that we are all those wonderful things. We are beautiful. We are enough. We are the light. When you have been in an abusive relationship of any kind (romantic, friendship, religion, work, etc.), those are not words that you hear, much less believe about yourself. When you are beaten down and told all the things that you are doing wrong and that you are not worthy, it's very hard to find that inner strength and know that that is all just BS.

If we can clear our mind of all of the clutter and tap into who we were when we were born, that perfect soul, then anything is possible. Knowing my conditioned and limiting beliefs along with my primary human needs, I was able to create a list of daily affirmations that I committed to becoming. I chose affirmations that guided me to acceptance, forgiveness, and above all else, to unconditional self-love.

I write these affirmations down every day in my journal. Along with the affirmations, I write down my goals and dreams—things that I want to become or create, ways to better myself. When you dream big, you must have a plan, and you must act. In addition to writing out daily affirmations, I began listening to sleep meditations at night to reprogram my subconscious of all the things I wanted and deserved.

In the Infinity of life where I am all is perfect whole incomplete. I now choose calmly and objectively to see my old patterns, and I am willing to make changes. I am teachable. I can learn. I am willing to change. I choose to have fun doing this. I choose to react as though I have found a treasure when I discover something else to release. I see and feel myself changing moment by moment. Thoughts no longer have any power over me. I am the power in the world I choose to be free. All is well in my world.

—Louis Hay, *You Can Heal Your Life*

I remember listening to a YouTube video by Marisa Peer, titled "Stop Negative Thinking—How to Master Your Negative Thoughts and Use Them for Good." It encouraged me to write the words *I am love, I am enough, I am beautiful, I deserve the best* on my bathroom mirror. I wrote these words on every mirror in my home as well as the mirrors at my company.

The video talked about how when we see these words over and over and tell them to ourselves, it can shift our perspective. This is in direct contrast to being told we're not good enough or we're not worthy, we're not valued, we're ugly or stupid or any of the other horrible things that we have been told or that we tell ourselves. The language that we use to ourselves is probably more crucial than the language that other people aim at us.

Self-talk can destroy your worth or build it. When we can shift our perspective and treat ourselves with love, grace, and kindness, we can find our true beauty within. It will shine through in everything we do. Affirmations can be done in so many ways: you can write them on a mirror, you can journal them, you can record yourself and listen to it each day. The most important thing about affirmations is understanding this is about you changing a limiting belief about yourself;

this is about reprogramming the subconscious mind with positive thoughts and empowering statements. What you think internally becomes your reality.

I want you to think about dreaming. Did you ever wake up in the middle of the night sweating and breathing heavily? Maybe you were being chased in your dream, and when you wake up it seems so real. Then you realize it was nothing more than a dream. This is the reality of your subconscious mind. If you believe when you wake up from a dream that you are being chased, what would happen if you could change the subconscious mind to believe that you are enough, you are beautiful, you are worthy?

I challenge each of you to meditate on the limiting beliefs you have and figure out how you need to change those words to a more empowering positive thought process. Write those affirmations on all your mirrors so that every time you pass by that mirror, you are subconsciously reading those positive thoughts. Mel Robbins, an author, encourages you to give yourself a high five each time you walk in front of a mirror. Think about that for a second. When someone gives you a high five, you get a burst of serotonin and dopamine. You can do this yourself every day.

It is up to you to control the thoughts in your brain. It is up to you to change your perspective. You have a beautiful light within you that is meant to shine. You are enough.

Chapter 7

The Power of Forgiveness

It's not an easy journey, to get to a place
where you forgive people. But it is such a
powerful place because it frees you.

—Tyler Perry

The day I lost my innocence, I woke up to an unimaginable horror—being touched in a way that felt wrong, yet I couldn't fully comprehend what was happening. Fear gripped me as I tried to speak, only to be silenced by a finger pressed to my lips. What followed was a moment of unexpected chaos: the man's wife, lying next to me, awoke, yanked me out of bed, threw a sheet over me, and began screaming at him. I kept my eyes tightly shut, but I could hear her hitting him, throwing things, demanding to know what he thought he was doing.

She scooped me up, took me to the living room, and promised that he would never touch me again. She told me it was all just a bad dream, but also that I could never tell anyone because if I did, my father would kill him and end up in jail.

As a nine-year-old, the thought of causing such pain and chaos was too much to bear. So I buried the memory deep inside, convincing myself it was nothing more than a nightmare.

Years passed, and I lived my life as if nothing had happened. The man never came near me again, and I managed to suppress the memory entirely. But at thirteen, the nightmares started. I confided in a woman from our church, hoping for guidance, only to be told that it was all in my head—a figment of my imagination. She convinced me that none of it was real, and even if it was, I had to protect my father. So once again, I buried the truth, trying to convince myself it was just a bad dream.

Years later, during my first marriage, the flashbacks began. Therapy revealed that the nightmare was, in fact, real. When I finally told my mother, she struggled to believe me, suggesting that perhaps the therapist had planted the memory in my mind. But over time, and through more open conversations, my mother came to believe and support me, expressing deep regret for not protecting me.

As I uncovered more of the truth, I learned that the woman in the church who had dismissed my trauma had a son who was a known child molester. She had convinced me it was just a dream to protect someone who was doing the same thing her son had done to others. Understanding this revelation added another layer of complexity to my healing process.

I knew I had to confront all the demons that had haunted me. I wanted to be loved, but more importantly, I wanted to love myself. As I continued to heal, the old wound kept resurfacing. I decided it was time to seek justice. But when

I approached a friend who worked in the sexual crimes and molestation division, I was devastated to learn that the statute of limitations had expired just two years earlier because there had been no penetration. The sense of betrayal by the justice system was overwhelming.

How could I possibly forgive the man who molested me? How could I forgive the people who failed to protect me, or the justice system that denied me closure? Forgiveness seemed impossible, but I realized it was necessary for my own healing. Letting go of the need to be right, the anger, and the desire for justice became crucial steps in moving forward.

I began exploring Reiki shortly after the loss of my baby sister, not realizing it would lead me on a journey to heal my inner child and learn to forgive. Reiki became a vital part of my therapy, helping me confront the deep wounds from my past. Being molested had a significant impact on how I navigated relationships, often in unhealthy ways. During my very first Reiki session, my Reiki master identified the pain I was carrying and guided me through a cord-cutting ritual to release it. As the sessions continued over the next year, more buried emotions began to surface.

My default coping mechanism has always been deletion—erasing every trace of painful experiences from my memory, or so I thought. It's like the saying, "You're dead to me." I would bury the memories so deep, it was as if they never existed. This included erasing every physical reminder of those who hurt me.

Through energy work and hypnosis, I was able to confront my molestation and sexual trauma along with the mental, verbal, and physical abuse I had endured. Reiki and hypnosis helped me find inner peace and begin the process of forgiveness. Now I embrace and love all parts of myself.

Forgiveness is not something that happens overnight, nor does it come automatically when someone apologizes. It's a deeply personal process that requires introspection, therapy, and a commitment to healing. I had tried to forgive in the past, but anger, shame, guilt, and judgment always lingered in the background.

Anger

Anger is a natural response to feeling wronged, betrayed, and hurt. For many years, anger was my protective mechanism, keeping people at a distance so they couldn't hurt me. But as I grew older, I realized that I didn't want to become an angry, resentful person. I wanted to be happy, to be surrounded by happiness. Releasing anger meant changing the narrative in my head and letting go of the story I had told myself and others.

For years, I had replayed the painful events, seeking validation from others to justify my anger. But in doing so, I was only fueling the fire. I needed to be right, to have others agree with me, so I could avoid confronting the deeper emotions of shame, guilt, and judgment. But holding on to anger only kept me stuck in a cycle of pain. I had come to a crossroad. It was time to face all of the emotions head on.

Shame

Shame is a powerful emotion, often too much for a child to bear. As I buried the trauma over the years, I also buried the shame—the feeling that I had done something to deserve it, that people would think I was at fault. I feared that others would see my shame, that they knew I was dirty, unworthy.

A few years ago, I reconnected with a friend of mine from high school. When we started talking, he said, "You are so different."

Laughing, I replied, "We're all different."

He said, "No, in high school, you were this quiet girl who didn't say anything."

This wasn't the first time I had heard that from someone I had gone to school with. In high school, I was quiet and withdrawn, trying to avoid attention because I didn't want anyone to see the shame I carried. I felt different because of my upbringing in a strict religious environment, and the shame of being different only added to my silence.

As I grew older and experienced failed marriages, the shame deepened. I endured more than I should have because I was so concerned about what others would think. But through my healing journey, I've learned that I have nothing to be ashamed of. How can I hold on to shame for something that I had no control over? What happened to me was not my fault, and no one has the right to hurt or violate another person.

Judgment

Judgment is another layer of the emotional burden I carried. We all judge others and ourselves, often based on societal, familial, or religious beliefs. But I realized that judgment is often a reflection of something we dislike or fear within ourselves. Letting go of judgment requires surrender and acceptance—of ourselves, of others, and of the past.

Gabrielle Bernstein wrote, "Surrender requires acceptance of the past, presence in the moment, and faith in the future." To stop judging ourselves and others, we must first become aware of our judgments. Once we acknowledge them, we can explore the underlying reasons and begin to heal.

Judgment Detox, another book by Gabrielle Bernstein, offers an exercise in which you write down your judgments and reflect on them. The following are activity questions from her book:

• Are there any patterns in your judgment?
• Did anything you uncover surprise you?
• How does it make you feel to witness your judgment?
• Did you judge yourself for your own judgment? Did it bring you relief to look at the judgment? Did it make you uncomfortable to look at the judgment?

This process of witnessing your judgments can bring relief and help you let go of the negative emotions attached to them. "Bless it and release It."

Guilt

Shame and judgment often lead to guilt—the feeling that we've done something wrong or failed to do something we should have. I felt guilty because I *"allowed"* someone to touch me. I felt guilty because I didn't make someone *hear me.* I felt guilty because I stayed *quiet when I was told to.* I felt guilty because I thought I would be a disappointment to my family. The beliefs and reasons can go on and on.

Through my journey with Neuro-Linguistic Programming (NLP), I've been able to define and release the core, limiting, and conditioned beliefs that contributed to my guilt. I no longer take on beliefs that don't align with my true self. Awareness has been key to breaking free from these patterns. I know I have nothing to feel guilty for.

Forgiveness

It wasn't until recently that I truly understood what forgiveness is. Forgiveness is about choosing love over anger, acceptance over resistance. It's about loving all parts of myself, including the mistakes and the pain. I've learned that the wrongdoings of others have nothing to do with me but are a reflection of their own pain and struggle.

Forgiveness is not about excusing the behavior of those who hurt me, but about freeing myself from the burden of carrying that pain. It's about accepting my faults, learning from them, and growing into the person I am meant to be.

As Don Miguel Ruiz wrote in *Mastery of Love,* "the truth

is that we cannot forgive because you learn not to forgive, because you practice not to forgive, because you mastered not to forgive. Our personal importance grows when we do not forgive."

Over the last two years, I've discovered forgiveness for the broken relationships, judgments, and traumas I've experienced. Life isn't perfect, and there are still days when anger surfaces, but I now choose to approach it with love. I refuse to be a victim or to let anger control my life. When I feel triggered, I breathe, bless the moment, and release it.

Writing letters to those who have hurt me, journaling, meditation, Reiki, and hypnosis have all been powerful tools in my journey toward forgiveness. These practices aren't about blaming others or defending myself—they're about releasing the emotions and moving forward.

A New Perspective

Change your story change your life.

—Tony Robbins

As I've healed, I've begun to see each situation from a different perspective. The Perceptual Positions technique in Neuro-Linguistic Programming (NLP) has been particularly helpful in this regard, allowing me to see things from my perspective, the perspective of others, and that of an outside observer. This process allowed me to role-play, step into each role, feel what they were feeling, see what they were seeing, and live in it just as that person was. This process has helped me let go of anger and embrace a more compassionate, loving view of myself and others. When you can step into an event without judgment and go through the different perspectives, it will free your mind.

Another technique that has supported my healing is the Screen of Mind. This exercise allows me to take the hurt and anger and reframe it as a movie, shrinking the negative memories and replacing them with positive, empowering images. You are the star in the movie. You start out with breath work to get yourself into a calm state. Then you see yourself in this movie. All aspects of the experience are in bright color.

Now start shrinking this movie in your mind and turn the memories into a black-and-white movie. Now float into the future and see yourself in a new movie. Imagine how you want to be, feel, do. Make this image bigger and brighter. Live in the moment. Feel all the positive emotions, thoughts, joy, and happiness. Learning to see things through a different lens has been freeing. I have learned how to take an event or experience in my life and look at it from an empowering place.

This technique is very effective in changing a negative memory into a positive. Yes, the memory is still there; however, it is no longer dictating your state of mind or your every move. It's all about reframing the event. The technique should be performed by a licensed practitioner who can guide you through the process; what I have described is a condensed version of the actual process.

Forgiveness is ultimately about healing yourself. I choose to approach each day with love, gratitude, and kindness, refusing to let past hurts define who I am. The people who have hurt me were likely hurting themselves, and I pray for their peace.

But most importantly, I've learned to forgive myself, to love myself unconditionally, and to live my life to the fullest.

When we bring our shadows to light,
then they can be healed.

—Gabrielle Bernstein

Chapter 8

The Power of Your Inner Circle: Building a Team for Personal and Professional Growth

Throughout my life, I've realized the profound impact that surrounding yourself with the right people can have on your journey. Two of my favorite sayings are, "Show me your friends and I will show you your future" and "If your circle of friends do not inspire you, then you're in the wrong circle." My first encounter with this concept was during my time competing in beauty pageants. I had a coach for every aspect—public speaking, fitness, modeling—each one guiding me to excel in my pursuit of the crown. This early experience taught me the value of mentorship and the importance of being intentional about who you allow into your inner circle.

As I transitioned into the business world, this lesson became even more relevant. I made it a point to seek out those who were not only successful in my industry but also aligned with my values and aspirations. I hired a business coach, sought out mentors, and immersed myself in learning their behaviors, systems, and routines. This approach didn't just help me grow my business; it gave me the confidence to become an effective leader. I understood that if I wanted to be the best version of myself, I needed to surround myself with a "power team"—a group of people who support, love, and hold me accountable. These are not just friends or family members but individuals who push me to achieve my fullest potential, guiding me on the path to fulfilling my purpose and realizing my dreams.

Let me introduce you to my Power Team:

- **Joe Robertson, therapeutic fitness trainer.** Joe isn't just about physical fitness; he integrates the power of the mind into every aspect of training. He designs my workouts and meal plans, and helps me connect mental strength with physical endurance. My physical health is a priority, and with Joe's guidance, I'm not just staying fit—I'm staying sharp, energetic, and confident. His role is crucial in keeping me aligned with my goal of living a long, healthy life, and he never hesitates to push me when I'm not giving my all. Joe knows my dreams and helps me stay in peak condition so I can achieve them.
- **Jennifer Culverhouse, enneagram leadership coach.** Jennifer challenges me to step out of my comfort zone and embrace my softer side. Through her guidance, I've healed past wounds and now see a future where I can empower others from a place of calm and compassion. Jennifer introduced me to the concept of

white space—time with nothing on the schedule, just for me to be present, explore new things, or simply relax. This practice has become a cornerstone of my weekly routine, allowing me to recharge and maintain my peace. Jennifer's mantra "Softness is my greatest strength" has become a guiding principle in my life.

- **Stacie Uling, Tony Robbins coach.** Stacie is my anchor in maintaining harmony between work and life. Her guidance keeps me focused and productive, whether I'm tackling work tasks, nurturing relationships, or pursuing personal goals. She constantly challenges my perspective, helping me see and approach situations differently. Stacie also helps me create an RPM (Results, Purpose, Massive Action) plan, a strategic roadmap to achieve my goals. Her encouragement and accountability have been instrumental in my success.

- **Deb McMahn, business coach, mentor, and friend.** Deb is my reality check. She's the one who calls me out when I need to face hard truths. What started as a business relationship evolved into a deep mentorship and friendship. Deb stands by me in every battle, whether it's internal or external, pushing me to grow as a leader, business owner, and individual. Her guidance has been invaluable in building my dream salon team and achieving financial success. Deb, thank you for your unwavering support and for helping me become a better version of myself.

- **Ayla, spiritual advisor/Reiki master.** Ayla helps me stay grounded and process past traumas. Through Reiki sessions and hypnosis, she's guided me in releasing pain, guilt, and judgment, allowing me to find balance and peace in my life. Ayla has also introduced me to the power of chakras and energy, which has been a blessing in my personal growth. Under her guidance, I even achieved my first level of Reiki certification last year. Ayla, thank you for helping me find forgiveness and inner peace amidst life's chaos.

- **Rob Parker, NLP therapist and brother-in-law.** Rob's therapy sessions have been life-changing. He helps me identify and break free of old patterns that no longer serve my higher self. Rob is not only my therapist but also a trusted brother-in-law and travel companion. His advice and support are invaluable, and I'm grateful for his presence in my life.

- **Arristie Parker, my sister.** Arristie is my ultimate truth-teller. She challenges me to push higher and achieve more, always from a place of unconditional love. Her support and honesty are unmatched, and I look forward to many more adventures, growth, and awakenings together. Arristie, you are my rock and my wing person—thank you for always being there.

- **BB, spiritual advisor.** BB, affectionately known as the "crazy card lady," provides me with spiritual guidance and helps me listen to my inner voice. She's been instrumental in helping me release conditioned beliefs and connect more deeply with my spirituality. BB, thank you for teaching me to trust in the guidance of the Universe.

You might be wondering how to create a team like this for yourself. It's not about the number of people on your team; it's about finding the right individuals who will be your coaches, accountability partners, and cheerleaders. Your team will evolve over time, growing and shrinking as needed. Remember the saying, "You are the average of the five people you spend the most time with." If you want to change, surround yourself with those who embody the qualities you aspire to.

The Universe has a way of bringing the right people into your life and removing those who no longer serve your growth. Be open to receiving what the Universe offers, even if it doesn't align with your original plan. Synchronicity—when things just line up, and the right people, messages, or events appear— plays a significant role in this process. Trust in it.

When I faced challenges with one of my companies, I was momentarily lost in self-doubt. But a simple act of gratitude toward a client who was opening her third location reminded me of the importance of gratitude in my journey. My team, my company—they are incredible, and I'm exactly where I need to be. Reflecting on my goals and dreams, I realized that the turbulence I experience is necessary for growth. My Power Team is here to ensure I stay true to my purpose and values.

Last week, I made the life-changing decision to remove my breast implants after having them for over twenty-five years. Two cancer scares in four years were the wake-up calls I needed. The second scare, just four months earlier, pushed me to seriously consider the removal.

While I was discussing the upcoming biopsies with my sister at the beach, she shared a message from our sister

Gabby suggesting that I consider removing my implants. To my surprise, I had already been thinking about this for months. As if guided by some unseen force, my social media began showing me stories of women who had removed their implants, and two close friends shared their own experiences with me.

Despite my lingering doubts, the Universe continued to send me signs. At a leaders' conference, a friend encouraged me by saying, "Honey, you need to do it. It was the best decision I ever made. You will feel better." Four weeks later, during a conversation with one of my accounts, I learned that she too had just had her implants removed. The synchronicity was undeniable—the Universe was speaking loud and clear. The decision was finalized.

Reflecting on why I got implants in the first place, I realized it was rooted in the belief that looking a certain way would make me more attractive and loved. It sounds irrational now, but it was my truth at the time. Today, I am filled with immense relief and peace. I woke up from surgery pain-free, and the inflammation in my face, hips, knees, and hands disappeared.

Removing my implants symbolizes my journey toward self-love and acceptance, embracing myself exactly as I was created. I let go of the stigma I took on twenty-five years ago to look a certain way. The feeling of loving myself the way I was created is freeing. I am in no way saying that having implants is wrong. What I am saying is that for me, right now in my life, the reasons why I got them were not serving my higher self. This is an individual's own decision and choice to make.

Two weeks ago, a book fell off my office bookshelf. It was Dr. Wayne Dyer's *I Can See Clearly Now*, and it opened to two pages: "There are no accidents in this Universe" and "Attitude is everything in life." These messages were exactly what I needed to hear.

I share these experiences to illustrate that God, the Universe, or whatever higher power you believe in is always guiding us. We just need to be open to receiving messages. Synchronicity is a daily occurrence in my life, and I embrace it fully. Pay attention to the people who come into your life, or even those who leave. There is a plan for you, and the right people will show up when you need them most. Look for your Power Team—they are out there, waiting to help you achieve your fullest potential.

Chapter 9

My Future Self

It's been almost three years since I made the decision to divorce—a decision that marked the beginning of a journey toward self-love and personal growth. I opened my heart to both give and receive unconditional love, starting with myself. In the process, I committed to becoming the best version of me.

One of my coaches once asked, "What do you want in a relationship?" I pondered this question deeply before detailing the qualities I desired in a partner. Then, she challenged me further: "How do you need to show up to attract that kind of partner?" I realized that I had to embody those qualities myself. I needed to love, date, and be kind to myself, to understand that I would make mistakes and that those mistakes required grace, empathy, compassion, and unconditional love from myself. Only when I was willing to do that would I be ready for a healthy relationship.

Facing fear was the next step. *Fear* is one of the nastiest, most paralyzing words. I had experienced fear of getting hurt, fear of being vulnerable, fear of giving love, fear of receiving love, and fear of the unknown. Fear can disguise itself as protection, but it limits you from experiencing the life you deserve.

Over the past two years, I've danced with fear while learning to love myself. I've realized that a life paralyzed by fear is not truly living. It's not the life I want, and it's not the life I choose. I choose a life filled with self-care, confidence, self-worth, and unconditional love. I choose to open my heart and give love like never before—first to myself, then to my friends, family, and even strangers.

I want to feel the excitement of connection, the butterflies, the electric pulses that flow through me. I choose to embrace playfulness, laughter, and the comfort of another. I choose to fly free and experience all that life has to offer. I embrace the lessons, the experiences, the sadness, the pain, the joy, and most of all, the unconditional love. I embrace the validation that only I can give myself.

I trust the universe to guide me to my higher self. It's not about letting go of fear but rather about embracing it, dancing with it, and understanding that moving through the darkness is how you reach the light—the beautiful golden light that fills your soul with love, healing, and joy. It's about transforming the four-letter word *fear* into a bigger, stronger word: *love*. This is the foundation of a life filled with unconditional love, not only for yourself but for everyone around you.

I've spent considerable time near the ocean, and I know without a doubt that this is home for me. I wonder what life would be like traveling the world, exploring oceans everywhere. Could I do that? I met a man named John years ago who operates the umbrella and chair stands at my favorite condo in Florida. John works eight months a year and spends the other four traveling the world, exploring fearlessly and without limitations. Could I live like that—experiencing ultimate freedom, choosing confidence and joy over fear?

While I wonder about the future, I no longer live for it. I live in the *now*, because the now is all we ever truly have. When we think about the past, we do so in the now. When we think about the future, it's still in the now. Therefore, be present. Live *now*.

Making choices from a place of love rather than fear— that's truly living. Letting go of judgment, shame, and guilt, and replacing them with love—that's living.

We often hear that mistakes are good because they're how we learn and grow. It's true. Imagine going through life never making a mistake, never learning, never growing—just being complacent. How sad that life would be. That's a life not lived. Remember, with change comes growth, and with growth comes change.

We were put on this earth to experience both the good and the bad, to grow our spirits, to live into our higher selves, and to be of service to others. We must let go of the ego and embrace all that life has to offer—the good, the bad, and the ugly. It's about believing in yourself, empowering yourself, and knowing that you are loved.

We came into this world as love, and somewhere along the way, we lost it. Now is the time to return to that place where your inner being resides and show up for yourself with love.

It's time to see the confident, empowered, beautiful soul of love that you are. I see you.

Here is a beautiful poem that I was led to write while discovering how to love myself and others.

Laying Down the Shield

Suited up for battle, on high alert for danger,
They rise—they fall—they charge—they run.
Warrior mode equals survival mode, or does it?
It's time to release one last battle cry
and put down the shield.
True victory is not in the fight or the flight,
not in the number of fallen soldiers.
True victory is in laying down the shield
and surrendering to love and peace.
It's opening the heart to allow the
light to radiate from within.
It's allowing your soul to become infused with love.
The shield is strong and heavy; it provides the
necessary armor to protect yourself.
The shield deflects the blows, but it also keeps out the good.
Laying down the shield makes you vulnerable, or does it?
Laying down the shield opens you up to danger, or does it?
Go ahead—it's time to lay the shield down,
To be vulnerable, to embrace the good,
and to leave the battlefield.
It's time to let go of the scars and heal from within.
Laying down the shield, one last battle cry,
Only to embrace the true victory: *love.*

I am proud to say that for the first time in my life, I truly love *me*. I am at a point where I can give and receive love freely. As I enter the world of being open to a relationship, I am committed to the moment, committed to being the best version of love I can be to myself and others. I open my heart to give and to receive love. It's amazing that all this time, love was right here within my very soul. I did not need another human being to give me love.

While there are no guarantees in any relationship, there is a guarantee that we are made of love, and we are meant to give it freely. Love can and will conquer all things. The next time you question yourself, pause for a moment, close your eyes, and listen to that inner voice—the voice that comes from your heart. Show up for yourself with unconditional love.

Learning to love unconditionally is where I am now. Giving and receiving love without any expectations is a new journey for me. Giving love without expecting something in return is freeing. Replacing anger with love is freedom. I recently read *The Invitation* by Oriah. It's an amazing book that spoke to my soul:

It doesn't interest me what you do for a living.
I want to know what you ache for, and if you
dare to dream of me in your heart's longing.

It doesn't interest me how old you are. I want to
know if you will risk looking like a fool for love,
for your dream, for the adventure of being alive.

I encourage you to read this book. The inspiration alone is worth it.

I invite love into my life. I am committed to showing compassion, empathy, and love to myself and everyone else. My wish for you is to return to that beautiful, loving, innocent child you were born to be, the one who was confident, fearless, and full of joy and undeniable love.

Life is a beautiful journey filled with countless experiences. Learn to embrace each one as a journey of growth, forgiveness, and unconditional love for yourself. I will extend love to every relationship and experience because, without them, I wouldn't be who I am today. I wouldn't have written this book, and I wouldn't have learned empathy, forgiveness, or unconditional love.

May your life be a journey of discovering who you truly are and living into your purpose. May you honor yourself and your core values as a person. My wish is that this book will provide you with the tools and guidance to find your inner strength, to become empowered and confident from within, and to learn how to open your heart and love yourself. My wish is that you can forgive yourself and those who have trespassed against you. My wish is that you will let go of the limiting beliefs that do not serve your higher being. Release them and believe in yourself. Start living your life with purpose, love, gratitude, and grace. Let everyone see the real *you*.

To the Woman I Was, the Woman I Am, and the Woman I Will Become

I love you. All of you. You are beautiful, smart, kind, and worthy. You are full of love. You are enough. I see you.

Special Thanks

To my boys: Being your mother is the best role I could ever play in this lifetime. No, I am not perfect, but I love each of you beyond infinity. You are both handsome, smart young men. My hope is that if you take one thing from our mother-son relationship, it's this: You are enough.

Thank you to Arristie, Dawn, and Joe for allowing me to brainstorm the many ideas around this book. I appreciate your honest feedback, inspiration, and encouragement to take on this project.

Thank you to my family and friends. The support and strength you have provided me through the years is unbelievable. I am blessed to have friends who will show up at any given time to cry with me, laugh with me, or just give me a hug. Finding a group of friends who love unconditionally is the greatest reward imaginable.

To the people who have come and gone in my life, thank you. Thank you for the lessons, the moments, the challenges. Each of these has helped shape me into the person I am today.

To my friend who reminded me that "I am Jennifer *fucking* Boutwell," thank you for your friendship.

To my power team: You guys *rock*! Your mentorship, coaching, accountability, and support have been invaluable. Growing into your higher self is a daily lesson, and I wouldn't have received these messages and lessons.

To my Spirit Guides, Guardian Angels, Gabby and God: Thank you for always being with me. Thank you for showing me what love truly is. Thank you for giving me the messages, protection, and most of all, unconditional love. Thank you for guiding me to trust my inner voice as well as learn to use it for the greater good. Transformation equals growth.

Bibliography

Baron-Reid, Colette. "Meditation—The Beach-Joy of Being Found." *Apple Music*. Accessed April 2023.

Bernstein, Gabrielle. *Happy Days*. Hay House Inc., 2022.

————. *Judgment Detox*. Gallery Books, 2018.

Brown, Brené. *Rising Strong*. Random House Trade Paperback, 2017.

Buddha_Mindfulness (@buddha_mindfulness). *Instagram*. Accessed April 6, 2024.

Dyer, Dr. Wayne. *Excuses Begone!: How to Change Your Lifelong Self-Defeating Thinking Habits*. Hay House Inc., 2009.

————. *I Can See Clearly Now*. Hay House, Inc., 2015.

Harrison, Vicky. "12 Quotes About Grief." Full Circle Grief Center. https://fullcirclegc.org/2020/09/21/12-quotes-about-grief/. Accessed November 6, 2024.

Hay, Louise. *You Can Heal Your Life*. Hay House Inc., 1984, 1987, 2004.

Kern Lima, Jamie (@jamiekernlima). "Know Your Why, Then Fly Girl Fly." *Instagram*. Accessed August 5, 2024.

Lauren's Kids. "Facts and Stats about Child Sexual Abuse." www.laurenskids.org. Accessed April 24, 2024.

Livingood, Dr. *Livingood Daily*. Livingood Daily Inc. and Dr. Livingood, Revision 8.0, 6th printing, March 2004.

McGraw, Tim. *Grit and Grace: Train the Body, Train Your Life.* HarperCollins, 2019.

National Center for Victims of Crime. "Child Sexual Abuse Statistics." https://victimsofcrime.org/child-sexual-abuse-statistics/. Accessed October 25, 2024.

National Children's Alliance. "National Statistics on Child Abuse." https://www.nationalchildrensalliance.org/media-room/national-statistics-on-child-abuse/. Accessed October 25, 2024.

Oriah. *The Invitation*. HarperSanFrancisco, 2006.

Oxford Languages. "Courage." Accessed on Google April 6, 2004.

Peer, Marisa. "Stop Negative Thinking: How to Master Your Negative Thoughts and Use Them for Good." *YouTube.* Accessed August 2023.

Raypole, Crystal. Article reviewed by Alex Klein, PsyD, written by Crystal Raypole on September 15, 2020. Accessed April 23, 2024, from www.healthline.com.

Ruiz, Don Miguel. *The Mastery of Love.* Amber-Allen Publishing, 1999.

Shetty, Jay. "Let Yourself Be Alone." In *Eight Rules of Love.* Simon and Schuster, 2023.

Singer, Michael A. *The Untethered Soul.* Copublication of New Harbinger Publications and Noetic Books, 2007.

The Life Blog. "Self-Care Quotes to Give Yourself the Care You Deserve." Accessed April 2024.